Knife ~~~

with

Groups

Forest School Leader's Guide

For Susannah, thanks for all you have done supporting the development of Forest Schools through FEI

Knife Use with Groups

Published by:
Muddyfaces Ltd
40 Olivet Road
Sheffield
S8 8QS
www.muddyfaces.co.uk   0114 221 9617

This book is a guidance document that aims to help Forest School and group leaders realise the power and potential of knives. The information and ideas provided have been created to help increase the understanding and confidence of practitioners aiming to use knives with groups.

It is NOT a substitute for training and personal hands on experience. It does not attempt to teach specific knife use techniques that can only be learned on an accredited course and practised over time.

This book contains guidance that could be potentially dangerous. The author makes no claim that the information in this book is complete and it should be seen as support information to be used alongside accredited training and practical experience. Neither the author nor contributors can accept any legal responsibility for any harm, injury, damage, loss or prosecution resulting from any activities or guidance described.

Contents

Acknowledgments

Grateful thanks are due to the knowledgeable and experienced training providers who have given their time to ensure best practice is outlined at all times.

I would like to give particular thanks to:

Jon Cree - www.worcestershire.gov.uk/cms/bishops-wood-centre.aspx
FS training co-ordinator at Bishops Wood Forest School and CPD training provider. Jon has been extremely supportive and positive throughout this whole process.

Louise Ambrose - www.birchwoodlearning.com
Forest School training provider. Louise's technical knowledge was outstanding and helped me to apply this in a way practitioners would find helpful.

The Forest School Training Network GB
In February 2011 the network had more than 20 members from Wales, England and Scotland.

I would also like to thank:

Clair Hobson & Scott Woolsgrove - www.earthcraftuk.com
EarthCraftuk is a community Interest Company offering Forest School training and CPD Courses. They have provided lots of knife use and maintenance knowledge and in particular applying this to Forest Schools.

Rowena Kenny - www.bathspa.academia.edu/RowenaKenny
Take a look at some of her interesting research.

Finally thank you to all the practitioners and friends who have read through with a knowledgeable eye, made constructive comments and corrected numerous grammatical errors. This particular skill is definitely not my strong point.

Introduction:
Breaking down barriers

A good knife is the most useful tool that anyone working in a woodland can have with them. It is versatile and once competent, the user can spend sustained periods of time using the knife to carve and whittle.

Many practitioners are reticent about using knives with their groups. This is due to a number of overlapping factors:

- Perceptions about children and young people having access to knives.

- Lack of confidence about using knives personally.

- Confusion about what the legalities are about using, carrying and storing knives.

- Inability to find appropriate insurance to cover knife work.

Although tools are not an essential requirement of Forest School, introducing appropriate tools at the right stage in a Forest School programme can develop learners' confidence, practical skills and gives them the opportunity to achieve tasks and create items independently. The use of tools is such a beneficial part of Forest School; it is unfortunate that many practitioners do not feel confident about running sessions.

1   Why are knives important ?

As with all elements of Forest School, the emphasis of using knives is on the holistic learning process that the individuals are going through as part of the experience, rather than the need to create physical products.

Knives provide many opportunities for working creatively either through making a whole piece of wood into something else, for example, a butter knife with an intricately carved handle or through transforming a number of elements and working with other tools to create something new.

This Giraffe for example is made with a saw and a carpenter's brace but will require a knife to whittle the wood on the legs so they can be tapped into the holes.

A more complicated project could be making a puppet, using a hand drill to make holes and string to connect pieces of wood together.

You can use a knife to make something functional such as a toasting stick or pair of tongs or for a more intricate project such as a whistle.

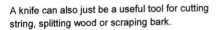

A knife can also just be a useful tool for cutting string, splitting wood or scraping bark.

Today there is much made of the dangers of knives due to the perceived increase in knife crime. However, if the skills are taught properly and effectively it will mean that knives are used safely, with respect and considered a useful tool rather than a dangerous weapon.

Holistic learning process

Knife work can aid fine motor skill development, hand eye co-ordination and spatial intelligence as well as increasing physical strength. It also provides an ideal risk management tool – competent knife users tend to be more aware of assessing and managing the risks associated with tools. To help you think about how using knives would affect your group fill in the boxes on the diagram below.

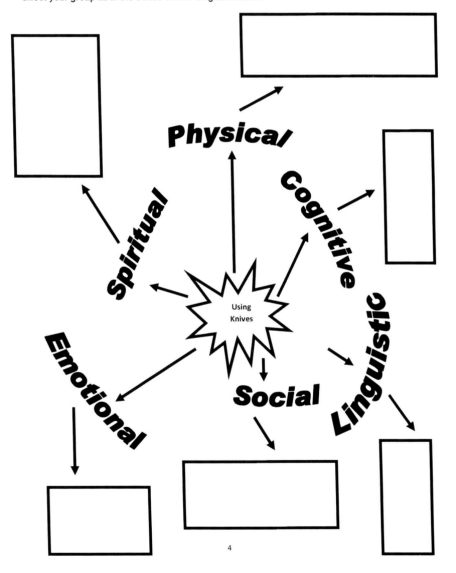

2   The practitioner

It is imperative that the leader running the knife use session is competent.

For a Forest School programme the Forest School practitioner is qualified to Level 3, they are responsible for the group and session. Any other adults assisting are doing so under the guidance and supervision of the Forest School practitioner.

Just because someone is qualified does not mean that they are competent.
A competent practitioner:

    i.   Only introduces knives when there is **relevant** purpose

    ii.   Is confident **handling and understanding** a range of knives

    iii.   Is an **experienced** knife user

    iv.   Understands when an individual or group is **ready** to use knives

    v.   Introduces the activity in a **consistent** manner

    vi.   Has **prepared** thoroughly

i. Relevance - is there a real purpose for tool use? Tools should only be used when there is a clear and relevant purpose that requires the use of a specific tool.

ii. Confidence in **handling and understanding** knives can only be gained through hands on experience and training. A thorough knowledge of the functionality of different knives is essential to avoid injuries. A breakdown of a range of different knives commonly used at Forest Schools is given in section six. This is by no means a finite list but it highlights a number of issues that need to be considered regarding different knives.

iii. Practitioners need to have **experience** of using knives in different situations, for different tasks and using different woods. This can be achieved by just spending time with your knife and different materials to gain an understanding of where a knife may slice quickly or get snagged on a knot

iv. Is the individual or group **ready** for tool use? Has the learner demonstrated the ability to follow instructions and boundaries effectively? Has there been sufficient time for the leader to build a trusting relationship with the learner? Is the learner interested and wants to use a knife? Does the learner have sufficient physical development for the task being introduced? Is it safe that day to use tools (weather, site, environmental factors)?

v. Introduction of the activity in a **consistent** manner. Forest School principles introduce children to new experiences through small achievable tasks. It is a practitioner's responsibility to pitch an activity with the correct amount of challenge to ensure that it remains interesting but with a final sense of achievement. Having a repetitive structure for introducing tools allows practitioners to constantly assess competency and encourages a deeper level of understanding and respect for the tools.

Example: Gradual and ability appropriate progression - part 1

Using potato peelers to peel vegetables is a good starting point – carrots and cucumbers.

Figure 2.1 Using potato peeler with support (because the carrot was difficult to hold, a glove was not used but a glove may be necessary when working at this stage).

Figure 2.2 Using potato peeler under very close supervision.

Figure 2.3 Using the potato peeler under supervision.

Figure 2.4 The use of this tool had a purpose – peel a carrot so it can be eaten.

It is imperative when working in close proximity to a child or adult that permission **"to stand close by and make physical contact if required"** is gained prior to the start of the session. The Leader should always talk through their actions e.g. "I am just going to put my hand on yours now to help you free the knife". This prevents the learner from having a shock when touched and keeps them informed. It also helps anyone else watching the situation to understand what is happening.

vi. Preparation - To give practitioners confidence and to make sure they satisfy the requirements of their insurance it is imperative to have thorough preparation before a tool use session.

- **a.)** **Risk assessments:** ensure you have read or created risk assessments for: site, activity, group.

- **b.)** **Personal Protective Equipment (PPE):** ensure that the correct PPE is available and well maintained.

- **c.)** **Staff:** appropriately trained and experienced, correct ratios for the age and nature of the group should also be ensured.

- **d.)** **Site:** when using tools with children the activity should take place in a designated area.

- Set up an appropriate number of workstations for you to manage safely.
- Ensure workstations are an adequate distance away from each other.
- Clear the site of any hazards.
- Allocate a position for the toolbox or bag and safety equipment.

- **e.)** **Tools:** The tool should have a consistent allocated position and should not be left unattended. Tools must be correct for the task, an appropriate size for the learner and in good condition.

- **f.)** **Materials** to be worked should be in an appropriate condition.

Forest School Training Network

It is imperative that practitioners wishing to run Forest School knife sessions have completed training through an approved provider and have become competent knife users themselves. There are over twenty training providers running Forest School training throughout the UK. The members of the Training Network are updated regularly on the FEI website www.foresteducation.org (Forest School section, guidance note 2a)

Example: Gradual and ability appropriate progression - part 2

Scraping wood with a knife – *potato peelers should not be used on wood* as they are not designed for this task and injury could occur.

Figure 3.1

Figure 3.2

Figure 3.1 Introduction of the safety equipment (glove not always necessary)

Figure 3.2 Position comfortable with stick secured under the arm

Figure 3.3

Figure 3.4

Figure 3.5

Figure 3.3 Using the knife with support. Close contact permission gained prior to session.

Figure 3.4 Using the knife under close supervision.

Figure 3.5 Intervention to help with a stuck knife; instructor explaining actions throughout.

Figure 3.6 & 3.7 Independent knife use under close supervision.

Figure 3.6

Figure 3.7

3 Legal considerations

There are many misconceptions surrounding the carrying of knives and tools with blades. As a Forest School practitioner, knives and tools with blades are frequently used either on school premises or taken out into a Forest School setting. It is important that practitioners working with knives are aware of the legal position in relation to the carrying of knives and bladed tools.

The Criminal Justices Act 1988 was introduced and deals with articles with blades or points and offensive weapons.

Under s139 it states "any person who has an article with him in a public place shall be guilty of an offence". This act reinforced the Prevention of Crime Act 1953 but it went on to define that it was an offence to carry any knife "which has a blade or is sharply pointed except a folding pocket knife. The blade of a pocket knife should not exceed 3 inches". (7.6 cm)

"A knife which is capable through manufacture to be locked open or has a fixed blade is thus deemed illegal in a public place." Although there are many penknives which have a cutting edge to its blade not exceeding 3 inches, a sizable proportion of these have some form of locking mechanism.

Under s139A it is an offence for any person, without lawful authority or good reason, to have with him on school premises any article to which s.139 applies. [Please note this applies to any premises, public or private (other than your own)]

A person who has been charged with the offence of carrying a knife or offensive weapon must prove he had **good reason or lawful authority** for having the item with him in a public place.
The acceptable defence for carrying a knife is to prove that it was

   a.   for use at work
   b.   for educational purposes
   c.   for religious reasons
   d.   as part of any national costume

This must be taken within context of that good reason/lawful authority, i.e. although you may have it with you because you are on your way back from running a session, it does not cover you to have it *on display*, for example, in the supermarket on your way back from a session.

Summary: - It is illegal to carry a knife in public except for folding pocket knives with a 3 inch blade (7.6 cm) or less, unless you can prove it is for work or educational purposes.
Perceptions

How could a practitioner's practice help prove that the knives are for work or educational purposes? Practitioners need to consider how their appearance and how they transport bladed items may be perceived.

A number of different precautions are outlined below. A practitioner could use these ideas (if appropriate to their circumstances) to make sure they are in a position of 'no doubt' in regard to transporting knives for educational purposes.

- **A written knife policy, procedure or method statement and knife use risk assessment** would show that hazards have been considered. The statement of pedagogy would put it into a Forest School context and show that there is an educational purpose for having the knives.

- **Wearing a uniform or having a card/badge** bearing an 'official' statement and contact information.

- **Keep a knife log** – Number knives and sheaths for counting knives in and out to ensure you have all of them before the box is locked ready for transporting and storage. This log could also be helpful for recording knife maintenance.

- **Transport knives in a suitable storage container** – Storage in a robust, locked box would show that the knives are being used responsibly and could not easily be accessed for use as a weapon.

  This box could also be used to transport knife maintenance logs so that they are always to hand if required.

- **A permission statement from site/ woodland owner** giving permission for the groups to be on this specific site carrying out specific activities.

- **A shadow board** may be useful for static sites to help store tools when not in use.

- **Knowledge of bylaws** - Have knowledge of local restrictions and expectations.

Example: Gradual and Ability Appropriate Progression - part 3.

Scraping the bark off with the appropriate knife for making a toasting stick or a dream catcher could be the next stage.

This can then lead on to whittling – A suitable wood is needed, with bark that is easily whittled either to a point (pegs, marshmallow sticks).

Then you can move to further whittling – fire sticks, mushrooms, decorating elder and ultimately spoons.

Example: Wands - decorated sticks

Figure 4.1 Knife held still, other hand twists the wood scoring the bark

Figure 4.2 Cleaning away bark between the lines, small accurate movements

Figure 4.3 Decorated wand

Forest School Insurance

It is widely recommended by trainers, FEI and the Forest School Network that

> Forest School leaders should have public liability insurance cover for their client group and planned activities. This is either obtained privately or through their organisation/school.
>
> It is worthwhile checking that your insurance company is a member of the Association of British Insurers (ABI)

A few insurance companies are recommended through the Forest School network. Each company gave a different response when asked about their insurance relating to using knives with groups.

Insurance company 1 gave a response outlining specific ratios that are allowed under the scheme for the use of knives, billhooks and saws.
This scheme is for Forest School practitioners and trainees with level 3 tutors.

Points to note regarding knives:-
- Use involving under 3s is excluded altogether
- For groups aged 3 - 12 approx, tuition is on a 1 to 1 basis
- Above this age it is flexible, but generally on a 1 to 2 ratio. Individuals must be supervised throughout.

Insurance company 2. The cover provided under this insurance scheme is in accordance with a practitioner's qualification and applicable health and safety procedures and does not go into specific details regarding activities such as knife use. It states practitioners should turn to 'National Governing Body' and 'Training Providers' for specific guidance/advice.

Insurance company 3 Did not insure tool use with children under 6yrs old

Practitioners need to be using tools as they were taught on their training course or as outlined as per their insurance. If they do not follow this practice then their insurance could be affected.
There is currently no specific guidance for different Forest School activities from a National Governing Body or from the Awarding Qualification Organisations (e.g. OCN, BTEC). With the lack of a NGB, responsibility falls to the trainers through the training network to agree and disseminate consistent tool use practice and information.

Woodland owners are advised to have public liability insurance cover.
If a charge is made for use of the property, landowners will also need commercial liability insurance. If there is no charge, it is recommended that they should ask to see a copy of the user group's current public liability insurance cover certificate.

4   Understanding Knives

It is important to understand your knives: how they are **constructed,** how they **differ** from each other and how they need to be **maintained.**

Having a good understanding about how knives work and the range of knives available will assist you in selecting the most appropriate knives for your group. If you are working to a tight budget it is tempting to go for quantity rather than quality. This is not an ideal situation as poor quality can mean rapid blunting or breaking. Where possible try to invest in quality equipment.

A good Forest School equipment supplier will be more than happy to talk you through their range of knives honestly, giving pros and cons for each while considering the specific needs of your group.

Knife construction

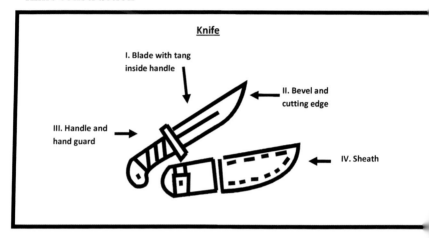

Knife

I. Blade with tang inside handle

II. Bevel and cutting edge

III. Handle and hand guard

IV. Sheath

i.   Blade & tang

Material – There are three main types of steel that a knife blade may be made from; stainless, carbon and laminate steels.

Material	Advantages	Disadvantages
Stainless steel	Corrodes less easily. Harder steel, so holds an edge for longer.	Harder steel, so more difficult to sharpen. Harder steel is more brittle.
Carbon steel	Softer steel, so easier to sharpen. Softer steel is more flexible.	Corrodes more easily. Softer steel also loses its edge quicker.
Laminate steel	Has the benefits of both steels above.	More expensive. Available in fewer designs.

If you're working with groups the stainless steel blade is probably a better choice. Stainless steel is harder, so holds its edge longer and is more weatherproof, but a bit harder to sharpen and more brittle (compared to carbon steel). Carbon steel really needs good maintenance regimes – which often doesn't happen with group or shared kit!

Blade description

There are many parts of a blade. The main ones are described below.

1. Blade point - the end of the knife used for piercing

2. Edge - the cutting surface of the knife extending from the point to the heel

3. Grind - the *cross section* shape of the blade (examples given in next section bevel and grind)

4. Spine - the thickest section of the blade

5. Fuller - the groove added to lighten the blade

6. Choil - where the blade is unsharpened and possibly indented as it meets the handle. May be used to prevent scratches to the handle when sharpening or as a forward-finger grip.

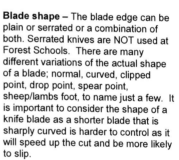

Blade shape – The blade edge can be plain or serrated or a combination of both. Serrated knives are NOT used at Forest Schools. There are many different variations of the actual shape of a blade; normal, curved, clipped point, drop point, spear point, sheep/lambs foot, to name just a few. It is important to consider the shape of a knife blade as a shorter blade that is sharply curved is harder to control as it will speed up the cut and be more likely to slip.

Tang - A tang is the protrusion of the steel into the handle of a knife or tool. The tang extension into the handle not only provides a way of attaching the handle, but improves the weight and balance of the knife, and adds strength and durability. There are different types of tangs: 'full' means that it extends into the full length of the handle, 'half' or 'partial' (Stick Tang) only goes part way into the handle. There is also file end or needle. The type of tang is important as it indicates how strong a knife is.

ii.   Bevel Grind and Cutting Edge

The bevel is the shape of the knife as the metal thins down to the sharp cutting edge. Bevels can be different shapes for different uses. A bevel can be on one or both sides of the cutting edge.
A few of the many bevels are discussed below to highlight how a different bevel affects a knife's suitability for different tasks.

Hollow ground bevels are not good for whittling work as you cannot whittle to the bevel and they are much harder to sharpen than a flat bevel as the cutting edge is a secondary bevel and harder to maintain. This grind can be found on knives that are used in butchering. This grind has been highlighted as it is very common on mass produced and often cheaper knives.

Hollow ground

Hollow Grind

Secondary bevel

Scandinavian (or sabre) grind is commonly used at Forest Schools on wood as you can whittle straight edges to the bevel and take off more wood.

Full flat blades are also good but the Scandinavian grind is much easier to sharpen as you only sharpening the flat edge up to the shoulder as opposed to the whole flat blade, which is a lot of metal to remove.

Scandinavian

Flat sides

Wide Bevel

25°

Children's wood carving and scout knives

Sabre bevel

Notice that the children's carving knife on the left has a more acute angled bevel increasing slightly the distance between the cutting edge and the change in angle.

Lambsfoot A folding knife with a very wide bevel very close to cutting edge. The blade also thickens towards the spine similar to a flat bevel.

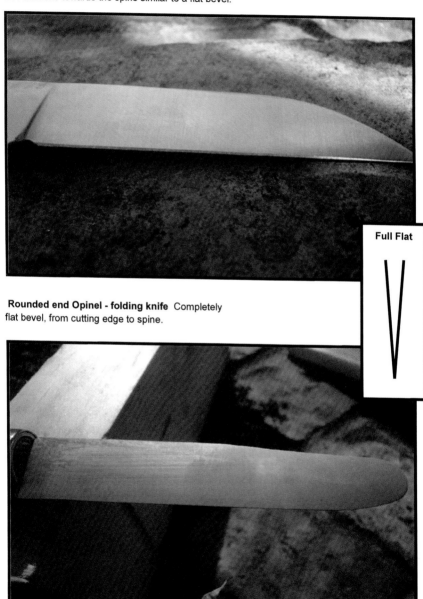

Full Flat

Rounded end Opinel - folding knife Completely flat bevel, from cutting edge to spine.

Convex bevels are rare in knives but do give the blade more bulk. They are harder to sharpen and are not so good for whittling as you cannot use the bevel and it is tricky to whittle flat surfaces. Convex bevels are stronger as there is more metal behind them therefore most commonly used in striking tools such as axes. The convex shape helps particularly in splitting woods as the shape forces the wood fibres apart.

Continuous curve from edge to spine

No apparent bevel

On the whole a bevel angle of 19-20 degrees on a flat grind is the best for wood carving. The wider a flat blade angle the more metal and therefore strength and weight behind it – wider angles are traditionally used for striking tools and narrower angles for throwing tools like billhooks.

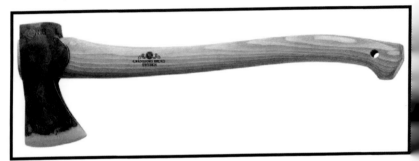

Forest School Training Network Recommendation
The Scandinavian grind is recommended for the majority of Forest School uses.

iii. Handle and hand guards

The handle is used to grip and manipulate the blade safely. The variety of handles is even greater than with blades and can be made out of many different materials such as metal, wood, plastic, bone and mixtures of different materials. The end of the handle or butt may have a hole to allow a lanyard (a thin cord or leather strap) to be attached.

The main considerations regarding handles are ergonomics and comfort. The size of the knife and handle should be size appropriate to the user. If handles are too thin or slippery they can be difficult to hold and those with a textured material around the handle can rub and cause blisters. Often handles that are chunky and grip well are better for children.

For groups that are more advanced and who will be doing a lot of whittling it is important to ensure the handles are comfortable and do not rub when used repetitively or with applied pressure.

Some knives may have a hand guard which is a barrier between the blade and the handle, protecting the hand from slipping towards the blade or something from slipping up the blade towards the hand. So are helpful particularly for beginners or students with different motor skills. However for more experienced knife users these guards can restrict the techniques that the knife can be used for, as the guard can get in the way or rub the hand.

iv. Sheath or folding and locking mechanism

Once the knife has been used it will need to be secured either into its sheath (fixed blade knife) or folded into itsself (folding blade knife).

Folding blade knives have a variety of mechanisms. Some require pressure others are spring loaded. The best way to investigate this would be to collect a variety of different knives and feel the different actions; this is also true for locking mechanisms. Some locks require you to put your fingers in front of the folding blade, others are twist locks and some are buttons. Folding blade knives are often weaker than fixed blade knives as the folding mechanism is a point of weakness and could fail. This increases risk of injury and will restrict the tasks a folding knife is appropriate for.

High Visibility – never lost. Sheaths can be clearly visible in a woodland environment.

5.   Differences between knives

Most practitioners, particularly those with little knife experience would look to source for their groups the same knives that they used on their training. This would make sense as they are familiar with them from frequent use on their training course. It is essential for practitioners to be familiar with a range of other knives and be able to access information regarding their advantages and disadvantages for use with different age groups. This will become crucial if someone is inheriting a project and the equipment and knives are not ones they are familiar with.

Advantages and disadvantages of fixed blades and folding blades

Folding Blade	
Advantages	Easier to carry and store.
Disadvantages	Folding mechanism increases risk of injury to the user either when opening or closing the blade or through a failure of the folding mechanism. Folding knives are weaker, due to the folding mechanism being a point of weakness and the blade not continuing into the handle as a tang. Could encourage users to carry knife in pocket (which may not be appropriate at Forest School).
Fixed Blade	
Advantages	Stronger than folding blade due to tang; this means that the knife can be used for a wider variety of tasks. Simpler in construction – no moving parts, so less likely to break or fail, meaning less risk of injury to user. Come in a variety of designs and often there is a choice of metal for the blade (stainless or carbon steel). Some designs include a hand guard to prevent beginners' hands slipping on to the blade.
Disadvantages	Could misplace sheath. Could encourage users to wear the knives on belts (which may not be appropriate at Forest School).

Knife variations can be significant and potentially hazardous.

Example: The knives in this picture have their cutting blades facing to the right but look completely different. If you are accustomed to using one type of knife and you swap, it is important to recognise what the differences are to avoid accidents.

The main styles of knives currently used at Forest Schools are:

    i.   Lockable folding blade
    ii.   Non-lockable folding blade
    iii.   Fixed blade
    iv.   Fixed blade with hand guard
    v.   Other knives

i. Locking folding blade knives

Example: Opinel locking penknives

Description: Opinel knives come in a vast array of styles, sizes from 4cm to 12cm blades, stainless steel and carbon, sharp point or rounded end and different coloured handles.

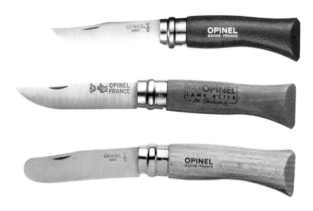

Advantages
Opinel knives are sharp and versatile, with a simple twist locking system that locks the knife both open and shut. The pointed end can be useful when carrying out intricate whittling.
The natural wood and simple design make the Opinel an attractive knife to handle.
The narrow angled flat bevelled edge can be sharpened to a very fine edge, ideal for slicing.

Disadvantages
These knives need to be kept well maintained and dried after every session as the wood in the handle can expand trapping the blade. This can cause problems when opening. (Tip - give them a tap first) The locking collar mechanism can be prone to come off the knife altogether. If this is lost then the knife is unsafe to use and must be decommissioned. As with any folding blade knife, the folding mechanism is a point of weakness and can fail during use. These are very difficult to use for whittling when students are new to them, as the blade is quite short and the pointed end is quite thin, so using the thumb and rolling action to do fine whittling is not easy. Also there is no choil so the finger can be cut if the hand slides forward onto the blade or when closing the knife as the knife blade extends all the way into the handle. The blade also has a flat bevel grind which is quite difficult to grind.

ii. Non-locking folding blade knives

Example: Lambsfoot

Description: This penknife has a bright orange, plastic handle, a straight Sheffield steel blade and has a hole for a carry strap.
It has a VERY stiff opening joint and no locking action.

Advantages
A stiff opening and closing action that reduces the potential of the blade being knocked shut. The blade folds neatly away into its bright casing.
The knives are full size with chunky handles. Often children find it easier to hold and grip larger handles. Mini or child size tools can often be fiddly causing frustration which can lead to accidents.
It has a choil (section of blade nearest handle without a cutting edge) meaning that if fingers slide forward onto the blade they touch blunt metal rather than a sharp edge.
The handle is bright orange for easy identification. If a tool is dropped or put down by accident in a woodland setting they can easily go out of sight in the leaf litter or soil. Bright coloured handles assist in their location. Coloured /obviously shaped handles also assist children to identify easily which part to hold safely.
The opening and shutting is not spring loaded which means it doesn't suddenly snap shut. The locking process is simple and doesn't require fingers to be in front of a shutting blade.

Disadvantages
The opening of the blade is very stiff and which can sometimes make it awkward to open. Practitioners need to be practised and competent at both opening and closing these knives. Most of the accidents occur when these knives are being closed.

Grease or oil in the hinge can assist with this. It also becomes easier with practise.
As with any folding blade knife, the folding mechanism is a point of weakness and can fail during use.

iii. Fixed blade knives

Example: Mora Sheath Knife, Stainless Steel and Carbon

Description: High-friction grip handled. The handle is covered with a layer of thermoplastic rubber for grip. This all purpose knife has a blade length of 10 cm, overall length 22 cm and a robust plastic sheath. Safety knives come with a bright orange sheath.

To put the knives away students need to be shown the runner inside the sheath which is for the sharp edge of the blade. This clicks in easily and ensures students do not put the blade in upside down.
It is best to hold the end of the sheath when removing the knife to avoid cutting yourself when removing.

Advantages - The big advantage of fixed blade knives is that they do not fold and therefore are stronger than folding knives. There are also no moving parts that could fail or be fiddled with. This Mora knife is half tang giving it the strength to undertake a huge variety of tasks. The knife is easy to remove and replace in its weatherproof, easily cleaned sheath. It is available in both stainless and carbon steel, with a variety of comfortable coloured handles and robust sheaths. It has a Scandinavian bevel grind which is the easiest to sharpen.

Disadvantages
If not pushed securely home into the sheath, or put in the sheath upside down, they can fall out of sheath leaving an open blade exposed.
Designed for adults, therefore too large for younger children to use comfortably.

iv. Fixed blade knives with hand guards

Examples: Scout and childrens' carving knife

Description: These two knives are child sized sheath knives with a leather holder with a clip to keep it secure. They have a metal hand shield preventing hands from slipping down the handle onto the blade.
Knife length 18cm Blade length 8.5cm

Advantages
As fixed blade knives with needle tangs, they are strong and appropriate for most outdoor tasks.
The smaller size of the knives makes them very appropriate for younger children.
Their Scandinavian bevel grind is the easiest to sharpen.
The scout knife is stainless steel which means it does not need the same level of maintenance as the carbon carving knife, but is more difficult to sharpen.
Hand protectors stop hands slipping down towards the blade.

Disadvantages
Scout knife hand guards can restrict the different grips for certain knife techniques for more experienced knife users. The scout knife upper hand guard can dig into the hand and cause blisters when whittling for long periods.
Too small for larger adult sized hands.

For whittling choose the childrens woodcarving knife that does not have the upper protector.

Forest School Training Network Recommendation
Many Forest School training companies recommended sheath knives as their top choice due to their simplicity.

There was an overall recommendation of the Mora sheath knife which is considered the best outdoor knife for adults to use. These knives might be too big for younger children to use.

The Eric Frost scout or carving knives were thought to be a better choice for younger children.

Both these knives are looked at in more detail in the following section.

Over time recommendations change due to new knives being available or a shift in opinion as the Forest School movement develops and matures. It is always worth discussing this with your training provider or a knowledgeable equipment advisor before you decide what you require.

V. Other knives used at Forest Schools

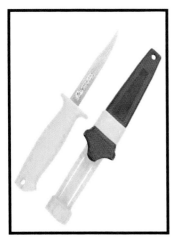

The Mora Sports Knife is more suited to **left-handed** users as the knife can be fitted securely in the sheath both ways round. It has a stainless steel blade, with a Scandinavian grind bevel with an acute point. The handle is slightly thinner than the other full-sized Mora knives, and would be suitable for smaller hands. The sheath has a retaining strap with a press-stud to help secure the knife during transport and storage. It can be used for either left or right handed carrying. The bright yellow knife handle and sheath trim means that it can be easily seen against leaf matter on a woodland floor.

Using a **Crook Knife** is a specialised form of whittling used to make bowl shapes in wood either for a bowl, spoon or any other bowl shape you may wish to make! The tool used is called a crook knife or sometimes referred to as a spoon gouge. It has a handle that fits into the crook of the fingers with a curved blade that can either be right handed, left handed or double bladed.
When using a crook knife the main technique is different from the normal fixed blade or penknife in that you need to cut across the grain.

Mora, Ray Illes and Ben Orford manufacture this type of knife. The Mora knife has a larger handle that is slightly harder to grip. The smaller blade on the Orford knife makes it easier to use for spoon work but is not as effective as the Mora knife for bowl work.

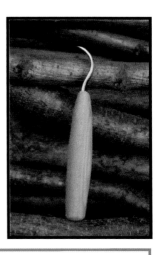

Forest School Training Network Recommendation

A single sided blade crook knife is safer to use than double bladed tools as the user is more prone to cutting themselves. It is also essential that the thumbs on both hands are kept clear of the knife – the non tooled hand thumb and fingers need to be protected by the piece of wood you are working on and the tooled hand thumb needs to be kept upright or on the tool handle (see the attached picture).
We recommend training in the use of the crook knife before starting due to the specialised technique required.

6   Knife Maintenance

It is important to clean and check knives after each session before the blades are protected (knives inserted into sheaths or folded away) ready for secure storage. When carrying out maintenance each part of the knife must be considered. Clean off all dirt and moisture and check for damage.

Blade and tang - Has it been bent and is there any 'wobble' between the handle and metal parts?
Bevel grind and cutting edge - Is it still sharp; are there any nicks, dents or scrapes?
Handle and hand guards - Are there any damage splits? (Pay particular attention to where the blade goes into the handle).
Sheath or folding and locking mechanism - Are the protective sheaths damaged in any way? Are the hinge and any other mechanisms free from dirt and working correctly?

It is useful to keep a record of knife use. A log sheet could be kept in the knife storage box so that it is always to hand. These logs are also useful to record which knives have been handed out. Alongside physical checks this log may also be helpful when determining when a knife requires sharpening.

Example: Knife log

Date	knife no.					Record of use	Duration	Comments	Action	Signed
	1	2	3	4	5					
10 Jul	Y		Y	Y		Heavy use - whittling	45 mins	All ok		FS leader
31 Jul	Y	Y	Y	Y	Y	Light use - cutting string	10 mins	No 5 broken handle	Remove from use. Not repairable	FS leader
4th Aug	Y	Y	Y	Y		Sharpened				FS leader

Sharpening knives

Knife sharpening is a skill that is only normally touched on during Forest School training but having a sharp blade is the most important factor to using a knife. A dull blade will tend to slip off the wood more than a sharp blade and is therefore more likely to cause an accident. It will also cause frustration and this could lead an individual to carry out possibly dangerous actions or to lose interest in their project. A sharp blade will penetrate the wood rather than slipping off and will assist in effective use of the knife. It is a practitioner's responsibility to recognise if a blade is sharp or not.

It is helpful for your understanding of knives to sharpen them yourself and progress where appropriate with your group onto tool sharpening. However it is a skill that requires good instruction and practice. Beginners, if not instructed correctly, tend to sharpen only the very edge of flat bevel blades. This produces a secondary bevel that can over time thicken in size, which can affect the effectiveness of the blade.

> **Forest School Training Network Recommendation**
> The Forest School Training Network agreed that the best stones are the Japanese waterstones – 800 and 1200 microns.

Japanese Waterstone
Waterstones are made of soft abrasive particles that break off during use. Each stroke with the blade breaks loose a small amount of tiny particles, which exposes new and sharp particles. The loose particles build up and combine with the water to create a muddy and abrasive slurry that helps speed up the sharpening process.

Oil stones are significantly cheaper than waterstones but are not as effective. Instead of the abrasive particles breaking off, they round over and become dull over time. At the same time, oil residue and metal particles can fill up the stone's pores, reducing the ability of the stone to produce a sharp edge.

Knife sharpeners. There are many different knife sharpeners available. The main disadvantage is that the angle they sharpen at may be different to the angle of the bevel on your knife.

For simple sharpening in the field of sabre bevelled knives it is worth looking at the Smith's two step sharpener.

Whetstone

Whestones have gained their name not from the lubricants used but from the old word 'whet' which means to sharpen a blade.

Sharpening steel

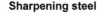

Used more commonly for kitchen knives

Sharpening stones come in a wide range of shapes, sizes and materials. They may be composed of natural quarried material, or from man-made material. Stones (water, oil and whet) are usually available in various grades.

Grades -This refers to the grit size of the particles in the stone. It is given as a number, which indicates the density of the particles with a higher number denoting smaller particles with a higher density. Finer grits with a higher density of particles give a finer finish. Finer grits cut more slowly because they remove less material. Other tools that can be sharpened with a sharpening stone include scissors, scythes, and chisels.

There are books, video clips on the internet, and online resources that can show you how to sharpen your knives. The best way would be to go on a tool maintenance CPD course or seek out a professional who can demonstrate knife sharpening techniques.

7   Consider your Practice

It is important that the group goes through a repetitive structured process to build up gradual understanding, expected behaviours and respect for the tools. It is useful that the same or similar sequence is used for introduction of any tool so that individuals can become familiar with the sequence of events.

A 10 step introduction to knife process has been laid out below for practitioners to consider their own practice against. This 10 step example utilises a logical approach but many aspects of it may not be appropriate for your particular groups or situations.

It may be beneficial for less experienced practitioners to lay out an appropriate sequence on a 'how to' card as a teaching aid that can fit in a pocket to ensure each stage is introduced logically.

This section is not designed to teach you any specific techniques but as an memory aid for aspects covered on your training.

10   step structure

i.	Introduction
ii.	Position & stance
iii.	Transporting (optional)
iv.	Passing (optional)
v.	Tool handling
vi.	Securing material to be worked
vii.	Basic use
viii.	Avoiding injuries
ix.	Storage and maintenance
x.	Advanced use

i. Introduction
a.) Briefly introduce the tool and task giving its name and use. E.g. "This is a penknife and we will be using it to whittle a point on a stick."

b.) Ensure whenever you hold the tool you visually reiterate safe use by using correct holding and carrying techniques.

c.) Description of the tool parts A full description of the tool is given:
handle, blade, tip etc.

ii. **Position & Stance**

a.) Physical position/ body stance. It is essential that a safe stance is used when handling knives. When using a knife the user's body position must be **stable. Hold the wood securely, feel comfortable and safe**. There are various stances that could be used that fulfil these requirements. The FS leader should present knife use based on the learner's age, experience, physical ability and dexterity.

b.) Self awareness. Position group members at workstations with a safe stance, safe distance and safe working area. This will mean the student will be working with the tool and then the information about safety will be retained and have meaning. Just listening to a safety talk will not work for most students as it has no real purpose at that time.
For safe working distance you need to emphasise the **'blood bubble' i.e. arm's length plus 1 x tool length**. Note; if two people are working their bubbles cannot overlap so actual distance between people is double = 2 x arms lengths + 2 x tools length. Other bladed tools would have different blood bubbles.

This process builds up understanding gradually making them aware of each other and also encourages peer support. How and when to walk around the site when tool use is happening, is also a valuable point to discuss.

c.) Safe distance. Ensure sufficient space between group members.
Use the 'blood bubble'.

Example: Knife stances used at Forest Schools.

Stance 1.
Sitting with work on the outside of the body

The safest position for working with knives is sitting in a comfortable and stable position.

The upper body is turned slightly which allows the item being worked and the knife to be out to one side of the body. This ensures that the knife is working away from the body (particularly any main arteries).

Forest School Training Network
Recommendation
Working out to the side of your body is the position recommended by the Training Network. It is the position of choice when introducing beginners to knives as it is ensures any slips or problems happen away from the body.

Stance 2
3 point kneeling stance.

This is a stable stance as 3 points of the body are in contact with the ground. The toe and knee on the same side as the dominant hand (the hand holding the knife) are on the ground enabling space for the hand to move as it works. The non dominant side knee is raised enabling the wood (remembering to keep the materials long) to be braced using the leg and non dominant arm.

The work is always held in front of the body, by ensuring the upper body is either vertical or slightly leaning forward.

Stance 3
Using a block on the outside of the body.

Using a block to work on can help keep the wood still and provide support as a platform to cut down onto.

The block should be on the outside of the dominant hand side of body (so that you are side on to the block, rather than it being in front of you).

Note that to protect the knuckles of the hand holding the knife you need to work towards the back of the block so the handle misses the block.

Stance 4
Sitting with wide legs and elbows on knees.

This is a comfortable position which is easier to maintain for long periods of time when fine whittling (NOTE this is not an appropriate position for any work that requires forceful cuts). However it is the stance that presents the biggest risk. Sitting on a stable seat, spread the legs wide, lean the body forward from the hips and place elbows onto the knees so that the work is in front of the body, well away from the legs and thighs. If using this stance it is essential that the Forest School leader carefully observes learners, as often knife users can slowly move their body back so that the knife becomes close to the legs or groin area. The femoral artery runs down the inner thighs so this has the potential of being very high risk.

Body Stance	Advantages	Disadvantages
Stance 1 Sitting with work on the outside of the body.	Work is on outside of body so less risk of cutting leg if knife slips.	Can be uncomfortable after time as upper body is twisted. Difficult to get much force behind cut.
Stance 2 3 point kneeling stance.	Work is in front of body away from femoral artery and legs. Very stable as 3 points in contact with ground.	Can be uncomfortable after time. Difficult for people with knee or back problems to maintain stance.
Stance 3 Using a block on the outside of body.	Work is on outside of body so less risk of cutting leg if knife slips. Using block as a platform will support the work and act as a barrier if knife slips. Easier to use more force behind cut and use the entire arm.	Can be uncomfortable after time as upper body is twisted. Can hit knuckles on the block if the work moves forward on the block.
Stance 4 Sitting with wide legs and elbows on knees.	Comfortable to maintain for lengths of time.	Can be a tendency over time for person to move back so that the work is over thighs – which is a very risky position.

iii. Transporting (Optional)
This is not needed if the practitioner hands out tools whilst students are at their work stations. The students are stationary and can get used to working with the tool. The tutors model safe transportation at this stage and then later on how to transport is discussed and the students can practise this. Tools should not be carried in pockets or on belts.

iv. Passing (Optional)
This should be initially between the tutor and the student and can be practised with eye contact and statements "I am passing you the knife". This ensures the student is paying attention and it also gives the students the model to follow. It also allows you to reinforce that when the knife is not in use, it should be in the closed or sheathed position. This will minimise the risk of accidents.

v. Tool handling
Safe opening and closing / unsheathing of the knife. Depending on circumstance some practitioners may choose not to do this and hand out the tools opened or unsheathed.

Example: Handling a folding knife.
Open the knife pointing away from you with the hinged end closest to you. Take the blunt edge of the blade in one hand and the handle in a pinched hold with the other. Pull the blade out of the handle, always keeping the hinge closest to you and the length of the knife pointing away. It should feel like you are opening a fan with the point of the blade and the end of the handle moving out towards the right and left, until it is completely open.

To close: Follow the opening procedure in reverse, holding using pinched holds the blunt blade edge in one hand and the handle with the other (never put a finger across the slot). Close the knife pointing away from you, one hand on the handle and the other on the edge of the blade, like a fan.

Hand out closed penknives and ask each member to open and shut the knife safely. You may do this consecutively or concurrently depending on age, ratios etc. The opening and closing of the knife are likely times for accidents. Take time to practise becoming familiar with a particular knife's resistance/spring action of the hinge. Collect in the closed knives.

Once you are happy with the opening and closing technique collect the knives back in. This reduces the number of things the group are holding and doing when they are learning a new technique, focusing attention on one thing at a time.

vi. Securing the material to be worked

Demonstrate holding a stick securely.

Place the pre-prepared stick under your arm at the side of your body, pointing forwards and towards the bench. Hold the stick about 20 cm from the end. This position gives the stick two control points making it more stable than holding a short piece in your hand only.

The hand holding the stick can have a protective glove on if you think necessary. With the other hand hold the knife.

vii. Basic use e.g. whittling

With the sharp edge of the blade pointing away from you, use long strokes keeping the flat of the blade close to the wood (shallow cuts) to shave off thin strips of bark and wood. Take the knife to the end and off the wood before beginning a new stroke. Shave off, or whittle, the exterior layers bit by bit turning the stick (never turn the knife) whilst gradually making a pointed end.

viii. Avoiding injuries

Make sure you can see all students and workstations clearly and that there are enough trained and experienced adults to work closely with the students. The adults should know where to stand to see the students.

The adults should know how to help students (from the side, just slightly behind) and this should be modelled. Help needs to be knife specific - If the knife gets stuck on a knot or goes into the wood at too steep an angle, the user may then try different ways to release the knife such as pressing very hard which could cause the knife to slip/fly out, or they may turn the stick and knife towards themselves to get extra leverage which makes the position much more dangerous. Make sure you are positioned so that you can see all the users, clearly identifying problems before they develop into risky situations. Encourage the group to ask for help immediately when they get stuck. They will then learn how to avoid difficulties in the future.

ix. Storage and maintenance

Once the session has finished all tools are returned to the secure toolbox. It is wise to count penknives out and in as they can easily get left on the ground or put in pockets. Before packing away check all blades are in good working order, any moisture is removed and wiped with an oily rag. Any damaged tools need to be labelled and either removed or repaired. Keep blades sharp.

x. Advanced use

Progressively more complicated jobs can be carried out always reaffirming each step through practise before progressing further.

At all stages of tool use, even when students/children are more competent there should be clear tool use at a designated area for using the tools and a Forest School leader to ensure safety and good practice. At no point should students / children be out of sight and working with the tools alone.

Advanced knife use

Once the group become competent knife users the potential for knife use is endless.

Further resources and information

Supporting organisations and networks
IOL Institute for outdoor learning www.outdoor-learning.org
/membership/forest_schools_sig.htm

FEI Forest education initiative www.foresteducation.org/

FEN Learning outside the classroom www.lotc.org.uk/

Forest School Wales www.forestschoolwales.org.uk
Tool use continuums and practical activities from members' resources pack. Forest School Wales is a charity that works to ensure that throughout Wales there is sustainable Forest School provision supported by a national network that will nurture the development of projects, offer advice, provide resources, guide best practice and provide continuing professional development and support for practitioners in Wales. You do not need to be based in Wales to become a member.

Bushcraft
Information and forum www.bushcraft.com

The Bushcraft Magazine published quarterly www.bushcraft-magazine.co.uk

Book - Ray Mears Essential Bushcraft ~Hodder and Stoughton.

Knife grinds explained.www.backyardbushman.com Further information about knife grinds.

Tool use and maintenance
BTCV British Trust of Conservation Volunteers. **Toolcare - ISBN 0946752249**

Book - Sharpening with Waterstones by Ian Kirby

Waterstone information www.hand-cut-dovetails.com/tools/3water-stone-maintenance/waterstonemaintenance.html

Knife sharpening Ray Mears knife sharpening video www.youtube.com/watch?v=We1-CDNaSFs

Guidance on law
www.basc.org.uk/en/departments/firearms/knives-advice-and-guidance.cfm

Time to go!

If you have a desire to write a Forest School Leaders guide on your specialised subject please get in touch. We would love to support you in getting it published.

Contact Liz
at

www.muddyfaces.co.uk

Liz Knowles: Whilst working as outdoor pursuits instructor and an environmental education leader for the Peak District National Park, Liz became interested in Forest Schools. The more she learnt the more involved she became and this was the start of an amazing and life changing Forest Schools journey filled with wonderful experiences in the outdoors. Now working part time at Muddyfaces, Liz can share this sense of excitement about the outdoors with her two young sons particularly on their Forest Friday sessions at her son's nursery.